of PLACES and THINGS in the BIBLE

Parents/Teachers Manual 1

of PLACES and THINGS in the BIBLE
Parents/Teachers Manual 1

BY
©Oluwakemi O.Ola-Ojo
2011

ABC of Places and Things in the Bible
(Parents/Teachers Manual Book 1)
ISBN 978-1-908015-02-0

© 2011 by OLUWAKEMI O. OLA-OJO
All publishing rights belong exclusively to Protokos Publishers.

Published by:
Protokos Publishers
PO Box 48424
London
SE15 2YL
United Kingdom.
Website: www.protokospublishers.co.uk
E-Mail: admin@protokospublishers.co.uk

Printed in the United Kingdom. All rights reserved under International Copyright Law. Contents and/or cover may not be reproduced in whole or in part in any form without the express written consent of the Publisher.

Parents/Teachers Manual

To:
My young reading audience,
their parents and teachers,
worldwide.

ACKNOWLEDGEMENT

I am most grateful to God who through Jesus Christ came into my life at the age of 8 and, the blessed Holy Spirit who has since been my Teacher, Friend and Mentor.

I am grateful to God for my family, friends and those in the various Children Ministries who have been a blessing and encouragement to me.

Thanks to my Editor, Mrs. `Sumbo Oladipo'. Her passion and dedication in editing these series has been remarkable.

Thanks to all who found time to read and comment on this book for their invaluable contributions and words of encouragement.

I am grateful J.Oredein, B.Diedericks and R.Maleking for being a blessing on this project and Segun Omotuyole for the excellent cover design.

Finally but not in the least, my appreciation goes to the wonderful team at Protokos Publishers for working round the clock to get the series published and for marketing my books.

CONTENT PAGE:

Dedication		v
Acknowledgement		vi
About the Book		ix
Aim of the Series		xi
A:	Ark	16
B:	Basket	19
C:	Camel	22
D:	Donkey	25
E:	Emmaus	28
F:	Fish	31
G:	Galilee	34
H:	Heaven	37
I:	Island of Patmos	40
J:	Joppa	42
K:	Kidron	45
L:	Lions' den	48
M:	Macedonia.	51
N:	Nineveh	54
O:	Olive leaf	57
P:	Passover	60
Q:	Quails	63
R:	Rainbow	66
S:	Sun	69
T:	Ten Commandments	72
U:	Ur	75
V:	Valley	78
W:	Water	81

Parents/Teachers Manual

X:	Exile	84
Y:	Yeast	87
Z:	Mount Zion	90

Opportunity to be 'Born Again'   **93**
Other books by the Author   **95**
Useful Websites and Addresses   **113**

MY ABC OF PEOPLE AND THINGS IN THE BIBLE

ABOUT THIS BOOK:

This series is targeted at children through:
- Parents.
- Teachers in Primary Schools.
- Teachers in Bible Clubs and Sunday Schools.
- Teachers in afterschool Bible Clubs.

INTRODUCTION

In learning to read and write in English, children start with learning the alphabet from A to Z. A good knowledge of this forms the basic foundation for future education and communication. In the same way, this book focuses on the A-Z of places and things in the Bible in a way that makes it easier for parents and teachers to teach children the places and events in the Bible. According to Romans 10:17, "Faith comes by hearing and hearing by the word of God" but how can the children hear if they are not taught? With this book, our children will be able to practice some reading, writing and drawing at the same time. As there are 52 weeks in a year, there are two parents' books and two workbooks for this age group.

Parents/Teachers Manual

This is the first of a two-part series. Book 1 is for the parent/teacher and the workbook is for the child.

We recommend the teaching of an alphabet per week and advise that conscious efforts be made by the parent/teacher to do the exercise with the child all through the week.

In line with God's injunction in Deuteronomy 6:1-9 and the promised reward in Proverbs 22:6, we need to train/teach the children line-by-line and precept upon precept.

Each alphabet has been written up with some ideas. We would recommend that the parent/teacher use only what is applicable for the child and pitch the teaching to the child's level of understanding.

In the workbook the same story is written in simple English for the child to read. There is space for the child to draw and perhaps paint the drawing and practice some writings. It also affords the child the ability to read to the parent/teacher. The reading could be done daily as a bedtime story.

Effectively it is the child's workbook and it is meant to reinforce what has been taught previously.

AIM OF THE SERIES:

- To offer the opportunity for parents to have structured reading story with the child.
- To offer the opportunity for the child to read from the Bible at an early age with the hope of getting child interested in the Bible and God.
- To foster parent/child bonding and good childhood memories as they read and study the Bible together.
- This learning opportunity is for use during the week as opposed to Sunday school learning but will hopefully, complement and/or reinforce Sunday school learning.
- To stimulate learning of Bible stories and places in the Bible.
- To provide reinforcement of what is learnt through the suggested exercises.
- To provide an early opportunity for the child to learn about God, God's creation, learn to write, draw and perhaps read.
- To provide an early opportunity for the child to become saved and learn to grow in the Christian faith.
- To provide forum for the child to ask questions relating to God, Christian faith, fear and how to deal with it, etc.
- To provide opportunity to be a Christian mentor for the child.
- To provide the child the opportunity to self-express his/her creativity in reading, writing, drawing and colouring.

- To provide an early opportunity for the child to learn about places and things in the Bible.

There is an accompanying workbook for the child that will help him/her in learning to read, write/draw whilst at the same time reinforcing the lesson.

GUIDE TO THE PARENTS/TEACHERS

- Take time to read the story ahead of each lesson and pray.
- Depend on the Holy Spirit after good preparation.
- Aim is to teach child one alphabet per week.
- Parents are the first and most important teachers. They are God's representative to the child so they should live what they teach.
- Ideally parents should know the ability and capability of their child and each lesson should be adapted to the child.
- Both parents if possible should be involved; perhaps taking turns to read with child.
- Children have so much to learn in their lifetime and parents can share their experience as they read together.
- Remember to allow time for child's questions.
- Praise child for his/her effort however little.
- The same lesson can be adapted to the age and capability of any younger sibling in the same family.
- Aim is to teach child one alphabet per week, reading the story with the child from the children's Bible.
- Use child's name wherever child is written in the book i.e. make it very personal to the child.
- Use the accompanying workbook for the child to read, write and draw.
- Use simplified versions of the Bible e.g. NIV if a Children's Bible is not available.
- Make the story interesting.
- Keep it simple and straight to the point.

- Teach each lesson at least twice in a week when used at home.
- Read the story at bedtime throughout the week to reinforce knowledge.
- Relate Bible lesson for the week as much as possible to the daily events around the child.
- Encourage the child to do some writing practice as provided for in the workbook.
- Encourage the creativity in the child as he/she expresses it in drawing and colouring.

A is for the ark, the first ship and the first Zoo.

Genesis 6:1-9, 17.

Points:
- At one time, the people in the world were wicked.
- God was not happy with the evil in the world.
- Noah was the only man that obeyed God at this time in history.
- God decided to destroy the world that existed then.
- God spared Noah and his family.
- God told Noah to build a big ark with cypress wood covered with pitch.
- God told Noah exactly how to build the ark.
- This ark was a big ship and was to serve as shelter for Noah and his family.
- This ark was also to serve as a zoo for a pair of each animal kind and bird species.
- Noah and his family obeyed God in performing this task.
- The rains came and the world that existed then was destroyed but the ark floated on water.

- Noah and his family, the animals and birds in the ark were spared.
- God promised not to destroy the world again with water.
- The rainbow in the sky is the sign of the promise from God.

Exercise:

- Help the child identify the animals and the birds that were in the ark.
- The world is still wicked today as it was at the time of Noah.
- God has provided salvation from eternal destruction only through Jesus Christ.
- Give the child the opportunity to accept Jesus Christ as his/ her Lord and Saviour.
- Let the child know that God is still faithful to His promise, up until today and He continues to spare the world from being totally destroyed by flood.
- Help the child to identify how he/she can obey God.
- God made the man and the woman, identify with child some male and female members of your family or in your church or neighbourhood.
- God saw that everything He created was good including child.
- God gave the child two hands to hold, draw, paint, write, two ears to hear, two eyes to see, legs to walk, mouth to talk, eat and sing etc.
- God has a plan/reason for everyone He created including child.

Parent/Teacher's additional note:

B is for basket, in which a baby boy was placed on the river.

Read: Exodus 2:1-10.

Points:
- There was a new king in Egypt who did not know about Joseph or the Israelites.
- This new king in fear of the Israelites made a decree that would kill all the baby boys born to the Israelites.
- It was at this time that a baby boy was born to a Levite family.
- The parents of this baby boy kept him because he was very beautiful.
- After three months they could no longer keep their son safely.
- The baby's mother made a basket from papyrus and plastered it with bitumen and pitch.
- The baby boy was placed in this basket which was then carefully placed among the reeds on the bank of the river where the Princess may see the basket when she came for her bath.

- Marian, the baby's sister watched the basket from nearby.
- Soon the Princess came to the river to take her bath and she noticed this basket.
- When she opened the basket she found a crying baby boy inside it and the Princess had pity on the boy.
- The Princess named the baby boy 'Moses' meaning 'drawn out of the water'
- The Princess immediately adopted Moses as her son.

Exercise:

- Together with child, identify ways in which under supervision, the child can help look after any younger child – baby brothers or sisters, relatives, friends or neighbours.
- Explain to the child the meaning of his/her names.
- Explain to the child what adoption means. Please emphasise God's love to all children including the adopted one. We are all adopted to God's family through Jesus Christ (depending on the level of child's understanding you may need to give reasons why a child may need to be adopted or why a family may adopt a child).
- Reassure the child of your love, provision and protection of him/her.
- Find out from the child if there is anything or anyone that may be threatening his/her life at home or school. Prayerfully and carefully address this threat. Seek matured Christian or professional counselling if need be.

Parents/Teachers Manual

Parent/Teacher's additional note:

C is for the camels that Rebecca gave water to drink.

Read: Genesis 24:10-20

Points:
- Abraham's trusted servant went on a trip to the land of Ur.
- He went with 10 camels loaded with the best of Abraham's goods.
- They travelled a long distance to get to Ur.
- Abraham's servant made the camels to kneel down by the well outside the city in the evening, this was the usual time when women came to draw water from the well.
- Abraham's servant prayed to God to know the right wife for Isaac.
- Rebecca came along and he asked her for a drink of water.
- Rebecca gave him water to drink and she offered to give water to the camels too.
- Rebecca actually ran and gave water to the 10 camels.

Exercise:
Explain to the child that:
- God has a wonderful plan for his/her life.
- God is happy when we help others, especially strangers.
- Giving water to a camel takes a long time as the camel drinks a lot of water.

- It is good to care for other creatures i.e. look after their welfare.
- God is able to reward us for our good actions and intentions.
- God blessed Rebecca because of her care for the stranger and his camels.
- Explore with the child how he/she can show acts of kindness to others.
- Together with child, identify someone/charity that can benefit from a kindness that you and the child can work on, e.g. raise money for an orphanage etc.

Parent/Teacher's additional note:

Parents/Teachers Manual

D is for the donkey that spoke to Balaam.

Read: Numbers 22:1-35

Points:
- King Balak of Moab asked Balaam to come and put curses on the Israelites.
- Balaam initially refused king Balak's summon and offer of gifts after consulting with God.
- King Balak sent to Balaam more distinguished officers and promises of more gifts.
- Balaam consulted God and in the night God gave him permission to go to King Balak but Balaam must only speak what God tells him.
- Balaam went with the officials of Moab riding his donkey.
- Three times on the way, the angel of the Lord attempted to kill Balaam, Balaam's donkey saw the angel and refused to continue on the journey but Balaam did not see the angel.
- Three times, Balaam struck the donkey with his staff.
- The Lord opened the mouth of the donkey and it asked Balaam why he struck it each time especially as it had never behaved in that manner before.
- Balaam replied that he struck the donkey because he thought it was trying to make a fool of him.
- God then opened Balaam's eyes to see the angel of God standing on the road with a drawn sword in his hands.

ABC of Places and Things in the Bible

- Balaam repented of his perverse ways and promised only to speak what God tells him to say to the Israelites.
- Balaam's action of going to King Balak was right but his motive for going was wrong.

Exercise:
- Discuss what a donkey is and its job – carrying people and things.
- Together with child identify how our actions may appear right but our motive may be wrong e.g. giving so as to be noticed or being nice to others only when our parents are watching.
- Explain to the child that God knows and sees all his/her motives and actions.
- Explain to the child that God hates any action of cruelty to God or any of God's creation – animal, bird or man – by any person.
- Encourage child to be conscious not to destroy other species unnecessarily.
- Encourage child to do God's will only.
- Domestic animals are often more sensitive to what the average person may not see so be nice to them.

Parent/Teacher's additional note:

E is for Emmaus, which is about seven miles from Jerusalem.

Read: Luke 24:13 - 35

Points:
- Two men were walking from Jerusalem to Emmaus on the day Jesus resurrected from the grave.
- Emmaus was about seven miles from Jerusalem.
- One of the men was by name, Cleopas.
- Both men were discussing the death and the news of Jesus' resurrection as told by the women to the disciples.
- Jesus joined them in their walk but they did not recognise Him. Seeing that they were sad Jesus asked them what they were discussing.
- They told Him what had happened to Jesus of Nazareth and the news of His resurrection.
- Jesus rebuked them for their unbelief and then interpreted to them, the Scriptures about Himself.
- As they approached Emmaus, Jesus pretended to be going further but the two men invited Him to stay overnight with them.
- As Jesus blessed and broke the bread at the table with them, their eyes were opened and they recognised Him.
- Jesus immediately vanished from their sight.
- Joyfully and in excitement, Cleopas and the other man

immediately returned to Jerusalem and shared their experience with the disciples and other believers.

Exercise:

Explain to the child that Jesus Christ is:
- Interested in all that concerns any of His followers including child.
- Listening to every conversation of child.
- Still alive today in heaven but has given anyone who believes in Him the Holy Spirit who now teaches such people about Jesus Christ and how to live rightly.
- Still able to take away our sadness.
- Give child the opportunity of making the decision to receive Jesus Christ as his/her Saviour or re-dedicate his/her life to God.
- Encourage child to share his/her salvation experience with others.

Parent/Teacher's additional note:

F is for the fish that had money in its mouth for Jesus Christ's and Peter's tax.

Read: Matthew 17:24-27

Points:
- The tax collector came to ask Jesus Christ for his tax.
- Taxes are usually used to build and maintain public services such as government hospitals, our roads, our clean environment, law and order etc.
- Jesus Christ had no money to pay for his tax.
- Jesus Christ told Peter to go to the sea and fish.
- In the mouth of the first fish was going to be enough money to pay for their taxes.
- Peter obeyed Jesus Christ and found it so.
- Peter paid the tax for Jesus Christ and himself from the money he found in the mouth of the fish.

Exercise:
Explain to the child that:
- God wants us, including child, to obey the law of God and of our society.
- God is able to provide for all of child's needs.
- God has more than one way of providing for child's needs.
- The way in which God provides for His children always involves our obedience e.g. Peter having to go to the sea to fish.

- God is interested in all that concerns the welfare of child.
- Encourage child and together with child identify child's needs and/or that of the child's family or friends or missionary needs and pray.
- Together with child, expect a pleasant surprise God's way in meeting the identified needs.
- Remember to praise God with the child when this need has been met.

Parents/Teachers Manual

Parent/Teacher's additional note:

ABC of Places and Things in the Bible

G is for Galilee, where Jesus Christ met the disciples after His resurrection.

Read: Matthew 28:10. Acts 1:6-11

Points:
- Three days after Jesus Christ's burial some women went to the tomb where Jesus Christ had been buried to anoint His dead body.
- They found that the big stone covering the tomb entrance had been rolled away.
- Jesus Christ's body was no longer in the tomb and the clothes were folded.
- All the women returned home in tears but Mary Magdalene stayed behind weeping.
- Jesus Christ appeared to Mary Magdalene and asked her to inform the disciples to meet Him at Galilee.
- Jesus Christ later appeared to the disciples at Galilee before ascending to heaven as promised.

Exercise:
Explain to the child:
- Why Jesus Christ died.
- That Jesus Christ died and was buried.
- That Jesus Christ rose from the dead three days later.
- That Jesus Christ always keeps His promises to us.

- That Jesus Christ is the only One that died and rose again by Himself.
- That Jesus Christ is coming back again for believers.
- That Jesus Christ is still meeting with children of God today wherever they are i.e. through the person of the Holy Spirit.
- Today Jesus Christ's presence is everywhere so we do not have to go to Galilee or a special place to meet with Him.
- Give the child the opportunity to give or re dedicate his/her life to Jesus Christ.

Parent/Teacher's additional note:

H is for the Heaven, the home for believers when they die.

Read: 1 Thessalonians 4:13-18

Points:
- It is appointed for any man or woman, child or adult, boy or girl to die physically, after which is judgement.
- For anyone who has accepted Jesus Christ as his/her Lord and Saviour, the eternal resting place is heaven.
- Jesus Christ told us in the Bible that He was going to prepare for His followers places in heaven [John 14].
- God and the angels live in heaven.
- Dead people who gave their lives to Jesus Christ while they were alive also live in heaven.
- Heaven is a beautiful place with no sorrow, hunger, thirst, sickness, pain, loss or death.
- Heaven's streets are made of pure gold and in it are many beautiful houses and mansions as well.
- In heaven believers will worship God, singing happily forever.

Exercise:

- Let the child describe to you the most beautiful place he/she has ever been to or will love to visit and why.

- Explain to child that no one knows when he/she will die therefore it is very risky or dangerous to postpone accepting Jesus Christ as one's Lord and Saviour.
- Give the child the opportunity to be saved now and assure the saved child of his/her salvation.
- Together with the saved child list the people child will want to see in heaven e.g. loved ones who are already dead or his/her Bible heroes.
- Encourage the saved child to share his/her faith with others.
- Encourage the saved child on how to live a successful Christian life in the meantime before death.

Note to Parent/Teacher:
Be prepared to answer many questions including, "Will a baby that dies go to heaven or not?" If in doubt consult other matured Christians on this and on any other unclear matter. Do not be ashamed to inform the child that you do not have the answer right away but will find out and tell child later.

Parent/Teacher's additional note:

I is for the Island of Patmos.

Read: Revelation 1:9

Points:
- John was on the Island of Patmos for some time.
- That was very far away from John's hometown.
- Though very far away from home, God still spoke to John.
- The angel of the Lord appeared to John and spoke with him.
- John wrote to the people in seven churches when he was on the island.
- John also wrote about things that will happen many years later.
- John's writing to the churches and to us is in the last book of the Bible and it is called the book of Revelation.

Exercise:
- God knows where everyone is and sees us all.
- God still talks today if we can quietly listen.
- God is able to reach us however far away from home we may be.
- God is able to use us wherever we are, now or later.
- God can make the child a blessing to others.
- With the child identify how he/she can be used by God e.g. by helping his/her parents, cleaning up the room, putting away the toys, praying for and giving to others in need etc.

Parent/Teacher's additional note:

J is for Joppa, where Dorcas lived.

Read: Acts 9:36

Points:

- Joppa was a seaside town *[Acts 10:1-6, 2 Chronicles 2:16, Ezra 3:7, Jonah 1: 3]*.
- Many ships took off from Joppa.
- Dorcas lived in Joppa.
- Dorcas was a very good woman who helped many people.
- Jonah boarded a ship from Joppa to Tarshish.
- Simon the tanner, Peter's host lived in Joppa.

Exercise:

- Let the child identify any seaside town he/she has been to or would love to visit.
- Together with child list the unique features to be seen in such a town e.g. boats, ships, shops, fish.
- Together with child list the possible occupation peculiar to a seaside town e.g. fishing, sailing, shops and markets because of the ships and visitors.
- Let the child know that a seaside town is more likely to be very busy but God sees everyone, loves everyone including the child.

- The child should not be afraid of travelling in a ship so long as it is safe to do so.

Parent/Teacher's additional note:

K is for Kidron.

Read: 2 Samuel 15: 1-30.

Points:

- Kidron was a brook.
- Kidron brook was just outside of Jerusalem.
- David and his men passed through the brook one day whilst running from Jerusalem [2 Samuel 15:1-30].
- King Solomon told Shimei not to cross the Kidron brook [1 kings 2:36-46].
- King Asa burnt all his mother's idols at Kidron brook [1 Kings 15:13].
- Kidron brook was used for burning idols and things that did not belong to Jehovah God [2 Kings 23:4].

Exercise:
- Explain to the child what a brook is – stream.
- Discuss with child the difference between a stream and a sea.

STREAMS	**SEAS**
A stream is more shallow than a sea.	Seas are very deep.
A stream is not as wide as a sea and it can be crossed with a boat if necessary.	Seas are a large expanse of water and spread across many countries. A sea can only be crossed by large ships.
Trees are more likely to surround a stream.	Sand is more likely to be seen at the seaside
Streams are quieter.	Seas have turbulent waves.
Some streams dry up in the dry season or become smaller.	Seas never dry up rather its water increases especially in the rainy season.
Sometimes one can see the bottom of a stream.	One can never see the bottom of the sea by looking down.

- Identify with child what things one could find in a stream – fish, frog, toad, leaves on water etc.
- Trees around the streams are always green and productive even in the dry season in the same way being a child of God and, a friend of Jesus Christ makes us fruitful all the year round.

Parent/Teacher's additional note:

L is for Lion's den where Daniel was thrown by wicked people.

Read: Daniel 6:1-28

Points:

- Lions were kept in the den in the time of Daniel.
- The den was like a caged area for the lions.
- Daniel was thrown into the lion's den because he prayed to God.
- The king was sorry for having Daniel thrown into the lion's den.
- God sent His angels into the lions' den so the lions couldn't kill Daniel.
- The next morning the king got Daniel removed from the lions' den.
- Daniel came out of the lions' den unhurt.
- Daniel's enemies were thrown into the lions' den for their wicked plan.
- The lions ate them immediately.

Exercise:

- Together with child describe the lion e.g. king of the animals, big, eats other animals.

Parents/Teachers Manual

- Where do lions normally live? In the forests.
- Where can one see a lion today? In parks, zoos, game reserves or safaris. Some of these places can be found in Kenya and South Africa.
- Let child know it is dangerous to play with a lion.
- Re-assure the child that though he/she may get into trouble for loving God or serving Him like Daniel, God will always keep the child safe and get him/her out of such trouble.
- Encourage the child to love and serve God always.
- Spend time with child praying.

Parent/Teacher's additional note:

Parents/Teachers Manual

M is for Macedonia, the needy city that God showed Paul.

Read Acts 16:6-12

Points:

- Paul had a vision to go to Macedonia.
- Paul took Timothy with him to Macedonia.
- Paul preached about Jesus Christ to many people in Macedonia.
- Paul set up many Churches in Macedonia.
- Paul often passed through Macedonia.
- The Christians in Macedonia contributed some money and gave it to the poor Christians in Jerusalem [Romans 15:26].
- The Christians in Macedonia supported Paul financially in his ministry [2 Corinthians 11:9].
- Explain to the child what a vision is – dream, prophecy, revelation, image, mental picture from God about a thing, place or people.
- Let the child know that God loves us including the child such that He sometimes tells us what to do or where to go in a vision.
- Let child know that God will bless us when we obey Him in what He has shown us or told us to do in a vision.
- Let the child know it is okay to tell their friends about Jesus Christ, how much He loves us and what He has done for

him/her e.g. God made him/her beautiful/handsome, to know Jesus Christ etc.
- Let child know it is okay to give to the poor around us.

Exercise:

- Let child know it is okay to support their teachers and pastors by praying for them, being obedient to God and them, greeting them politely and saying thank you to them for teaching them or for being their teacher or Pastor.
- If they can afford it – giving or making the teacher/pastor a birthday/Christmas card or on special occasions.
- Identify with child any previous dream/vision and pray with child over it.
- Identify with child ways in which he/she can give to the poor, e.g. share meals at school, allow poor neighbours to play with his/her toys, give toys away to the poor, send some of his/her pocket money to a missionary or ministry in need, pray for those who need their prayers etc.
- Identify with child any street or road or town or country that needs urgent prayers.
- Together with the child pray for this place and thank God for answered prayers

Parents/Teachers Manual

Parent/Teacher's additional note:

N is for Nineveh, the city that turned to God in repentance.

Read: Jonah 3:1-10.

Points:

- Nineveh was a great city.
- The people of Nineveh sinned against the Lord.
- God told Jonah to go and preach in Nineveh so that they would not be destroyed.
- Jonah ran away in a ship to Tarshish.
- The Lord made a big fish to swallow Jonah and after 3 days vomited him on the seashore near Nineveh.
- Jonah obeyed God this time around and went to Nineveh preaching.
- The king and all the people of Nineveh fasted, repented of their sins and called unto God.
- God in love and mercy forgave the people of Nineveh and did not destroy them again.

Exercise:

- Together with child identify any great city nearby to you.

- Explain to the child what fasting, repentance and calling on God means.

Let child know that:
- God sees everyone including those in the great city.
- God is unhappy when we sin and that the reward of sin is death – physical death and separation from God for the sinner.
- God in love is still sending prophets and pastors to warn us of the rewards of sin.
- It is okay to tell others about the love and mercy of Jesus Christ.
- Everybody including the king, queen, president, prime minister is in need of God's mercy and love.
- God will forgive and protect child if and when child comes to Him saying sorry for his/her sins and not doing the wrong things again.

Parent/Teacher's additional note:

O is for olive leaf, brought back by the dove to Noah in the ark.

Read: Genesis 8:1-12.

Points:

- The Lord destroyed the whole earth with the rains and the flood.
- Only Noah, his family, animals and birds that were with him in the ark were saved from the flood.
- Many weeks after the flood, the water on the surface of the earth began to dry up.
- Noah wanted to check if it was safe to open the door of the ark so he sent out a raven. The raven came back to him after many hours of flight.
- The second time Noah sent out a dove, it came back in the evening with an olive leaf in its mouth. This olive leaf confirmed to Noah that there was life again on the earth and that the flood water was drying up as expected.
- The olive leaf is from olive tree.
- Olive trees are said to live for hundreds of years and it is said that they never die [Judges 9:8-9].
- We get olive oil from olive tree; olive oil is very pure, much more expensive than other oils and there is also olive fruit.

- Olive oils can be used for cooking or as oil for lighting the temple lamps and, it was one of the ingredients for burning incense in the temple of God several years ago.
- Olive trees were used in the construction of the temple by King Solomon..

Exercise:

- Together with child identify the parts of a tree – root, stem, branches, leaf, flowers and fruits.
- Let the child know that every part of the tree is significant and has a part to play in the life of that tree.
- Together with child identify what each part of the tree does, e.g. roots look for water and nutrients from the ground etc.
- Let the child know that each one of us is important to God and we are like the olive leaf or stem etc.
- Let the child know that every child is like the olive leaf, valuable to God; confirming His mercies unto man and for signs and wonders.
- Together with child, identify at least one good attribute of child and how he/she uses it to be a blessing.

Parents/Teachers Manual

Parent/Teacher's additional note:

P is for Passover, the feast in remembrance of God's deliverance.

Read: Exodus 12:1-51.

Points:

- The Israelites had been in Egypt for over 400 years.
- Towards the end of their stay in Egypt, the new Pharaoh made them slaves and overworked them.
- Some of them were beaten and others were killed by the Egyptians.
- They cried to God to deliver them and He sent Moses to them.
- Moses' appeals to Pharaoh for their release were not granted, despite the many miracles done by Moses.
- God told Moses to tell the Israelites to get a lamb per family, kill it and put some of its blood on the main entrance doors of their home. They were to roast the lamb by fire, eat it in a hurry, with bread made without yeast and bitter herbs.
- That night, the angel of destruction killed all the firstborn of the Egyptians, both of man and animals but spared the children of Israel.

- Passover means the angel of destruction passing over the families of the Israelites without killing them.
- The Lord told Moses the Israelites were to celebrate this Passover as a yearly feast from then on.

Exercise:

- Together with child identify some family or national celebrations and what each stands for, e.g. birthday, wedding anniversary, Independence Day etc.

Let the child know that:
- God is angry when we make other people slaves.
- God is angry when we are wicked to others e.g. steal their things, destroy their belongings such as school work, dolls, toys etc.
- God will always rescue us when we call on Him especially if we are treated badly.
- It is important to learn to call unto God every time especially when we are treated badly.
- It is important to tell those who can help us to stop those who are treating us badly e.g. report the tormentor or bully to the teacher or principal, abusive parents to the pastor or teacher.
- Jesus Christ paid the price for our sins – briefly explain the salvation message and give child the opportunity of accepting Jesus Christ to his or her life.
- The Lord will always send an angel to protect a child who has given his or her life to Jesus Christ [Matthew 18:10].
- It is always nice to remember special days e.g. some family or national celebrations or days God did miracles for us e.g. protected us from an accident or healed us and give God praise on those days especially.

Parent/Teacher's additional note:

Q is for quails.

Read: Exodus 16:1-21

Points:

- The people of Israel on their way from Egypt to Canaan complained to Moses.
- They wanted to eat meat again as they did whilst in Egypt.
- Moses called on God and He promised to give them meat.
- He sent them loads of quails – small, low flying, very delicious and nutritional birds.
- For 40 years the Israelites ate manna in the morning and quails at night.
- When they entered Canaan, they started eating the fruits of Canaan.

Exercise:

Let the child know that:
- God hears everything we say including our complaints and murmuring.
- God will in His mercies and love grant us our request in line with His word.
- God has more than enough to meet our daily needs if we would call to Him.
- God is still in the business of performing miracles however small or big.

- God is able to feed us all through our life without Him running short of supply.
- Together with child, identify a pressing need of the child and pray with and for the child in line with God's words and remember to thank Him too in advance.

Parents/Teachers Manual

Parent/Teacher's additional note:

R is for rainbow, the token of God's promise that He will never again destroy the whole earth by flood.

Read: Genesis 9:1-17

Points:

- Noah and all that were with him came out of the ark after the flood.
- Noah made a sacrifice unto the Lord for remembering them and saving them.
- God accepted Noah's sacrifice to Him.
- God promised Noah never again to destroy the whole world/earth with water.
- God placed in the sky a rainbow as a sign of His covenant/promise with mankind and for us as a reminder of His presence, His mercies, His love, His faithfulness, etc.
- The rainbow is always like a half of the circle but with many lovely colours.

Exercise:

- Together with child draw and talk about the rainbow e.g. what is it?

Parents/Teachers Manual

- Explain what the rainbow stands for in the Bible – God's covenant with man.
- How many colours are there in a rainbow?
- Identify with child at least one thing to thank God for and thank God together.
- Identify what the child can give to God even now e.g. time to pray, read the Bible, praise God by singing to Him and telling others about Him.
- God loves it when we say "Thank You" to Him.
- It is also nice for the child to say 'thank you' to anyone who helps or blesses the child.

Parent/Teacher's additional note:

S is for the sun, the greater light to rule the day.

Read: Genesis 1:16

Points:

- On the 4th day of creation, God created the sun to be in the sky.
- The sun is to divide the day from the night.
- The sun is to be for signs, seasons, days and years.
- Although the sun is way up in the sky, it gives light to the earth.
- The sun rules over the day whilst the moon and stars rule over the night.
- The sun keeps the earth warm – not too hot and not too cold.
- The grass and all the plants and trees make their food with the light from the sun and in turn they give us clean air to breathe in (Oxygen).
- Unlike the moon, there is no half or quarter sun.
- God allows the sun to shine on the good and the bad people at the same time.
- Let the child know that God's love like the sun is available to all.

Exercise:

- Together with child take note of the local time of the sunrise and sunset.
- Check with child to see how many hours per day the sun is up in your area.
- Discuss with child how the sun helps us to count days, years and seasons.
- Discuss with the child how the sun is good for him/her e.g. makes him/her feel warm, helps in drying our washed clothes, gives him/her light to see where he/she is going, helps our skin and bones etc.
- Explain to the child why he/she should never look directly into the sun.
- Explain to the child how Jesus Christ is the Light of the world.

Parents/Teachers Manual

Parent/Teacher's additional note:

T is for the Ten commandments, God's laws for man.

Read: Exodus 20:1-17

Points:

- God in love gave the Israelites Ten Commandments to follow.
- They were to learn the commandments by heart and obey them.
- They were to teach the Ten Commandments to their children too.
- In it God said He alone was to be worshipped and obeyed.
- They were not to make any image or drawing of Him for He is not limited.
- They were only to bow down to God.
- They were not to use the name of God carelessly, such as in swearing.
- They were to keep the worship day Holy by serving God and resting and, by refraining from doing any work.
- They were to honour their parents and obey them.
- They were not to kill people.
- They were not to take another man's wife.
- They were not to steal.
- They were not to say wrong things about others.
- They were not to take other people's things off them.

Exercise:

Explain to the child why:
- It is wrong to steal or say wrong things about others.
- It is important to rest one day a week and what it means to rest.
- He/she should not use God's name carelessly.
- He/she should honour his/her parent and honouring parents include obeying them for as long as his/her life is not threatened.
- Together with child memorize as many of the commandments as possible.

Note to the parent/teacher:
Stress only the applicable commandment to the child.

Parent/Teacher's additional note:

U is for Ur, where Abram lived before God called him to go to the Promised Land.

Read: Genesis 11:28-31, 12:1-3, 15:7

Points:

- Abram's family were originally from Ur.
- The Chaldees lived in the land of Ur.
- Abram's parents, brothers and sisters all lived in the land of Ur.
- They were a happy family living in Ur.
- One day God spoke to Abram to leave the land of Ur.
- He was to leave his father's house, his friends and work.
- He was to go to a land, which God would show him.
- Abram and his family were to go to the Promised Land.

Exercise:

Explain to the child:
- Where he/she originated from.
- That God still talks today and He still calls some people out of their place of birth or origin.
- How he/she can recognise the voice of God – God speaks calmly. He speaks words and things that build up, not words that destroy. He speaks in line with His will and His word as

recorded in the Bible. God speaks gently.
- Why God may call some people out of their place of birth or origin e.g. to bless them specially, to serve God by ministering to other people etc.

And
- If available go through some family photographs e.g. of grandparents, uncles, aunties, cousins, etc.
- Help the child to identify how he/she can hear God e.g. audibly, in their dreams, through the Word and/or as he/she reads the Bible etc.

Parent/Teacher's additional note:

V is for Valley of dry bones, where Ezekiel spoke the word and the breath of God raised a mighty army from the dry bones.

Read: Ezekiel 37:1-14

Points:

- Ezekiel was a priest *[Ezekiel 1:3]*.
- One day God showed Ezekiel in a vision a valley full of dry bones.
- A valley is the hollow between two hills.
- God asked Ezekiel if the dry bones could live.
- Ezekiel said to God that He alone could tell.
- God told Ezekiel to speak His words to the dry bones in the valley.
- Ezekiel obeyed God and God made living people out of the dry bones.

Exercise:

Explain to child:
- What a valley is – a deep/hollow between two hills.
- What a vision is – dream, revelation etc.
- That God made everything by His spoken word.
- The importance of what we say.

And that:
- We can with God's help make things better when we speak God's word.
- That it is important to obey God.
- That God has not stopped performing miracles even today – relate this to any recent testimony that the child knows or you know.
- That God is able to change any bad thing or situation that we see to a good one for His glory.

Parent/Teacher's additional note:

Parents/Teachers Manual

W is for water, which Jesus Christ turned to wine at the wedding in Cana.

Read: John 2:1-11

Points:

- Mary, the mother of Jesus Christ was invited to a wedding at Cana.
- Jesus Christ and His disciples were also invited to the wedding.
- In the house where the wedding was taking place, there were six empty pots.
- Usually they would have offered the visitor some of the water in the pot to wash his/her feet when they come into the house.
- Then the wine for the wedding party finished but the party was still on.
- Mary told Jesus Christ to please help, she also told the disciples to obey Jesus Christ.
- After some time, Jesus Christ told the disciples to fill the pots with water.
- Jesus Christ told the servants/ushers to serve the water.
- By the time it got to the chairman of the party, the water had turned into wine.

Exercise:

Explain to the child:

- What a wedding is, i.e. a man and a woman coming together in the presence of God, their families and friends, to become husband and wife.
- Who usually gets invited to a wedding party – Priest/Pastor, families of both bride and groom and their friends.
- What a wedding party in your culture looks like.
- If your child has been to a recent or is going to a forthcoming wedding you might wish to go over/discuss that particular wedding.
- That it was important to have table wine at the party in the time of Jesus Christ like we have soft drinks/juices today. It signifies joy and happiness.
- God answers us when we call on Him even at wedding parties.
- God wants us to celebrate and have happy parties.
- God wants to be a part of our celebrations.
- It is nice to obey God everywhere we are, even at parties!
- Encourage and teach child on how to say 'thank you' to God and people who bring him/her joy or who helps him/her especially in difficult times.

Parent/Teacher's additional note:

X is for Exile, where the Israelites were forcefully taken into.

Read: Daniel 1: 1- 21.

Points:

- God gave His rules and commandments to the Israelites.
- God wanted to be their God always.
- God warned them that when they disobeyed Him, they will be captured by other nations who will take them away from their homeland.
- Exile is a place where you are forced to be against your will, with those in exile separated from their homeland, family and friends.
- The king of Babylon captured Judah and took many of the people to Babylon.
- Men, women, children and young adults were taken into exile.
- Daniel and his friends too were taken into exile.

Exercise:

Explain to the child

- God has given us Ten Commandments to follow.

- Jesus summed the commandments into two – that we love God with all of our heart, soul and mind and that we should our neighbour like our self [Mark 12:30-31].
- God wants to be child's God always.
- Disobeying God is sin and sin will always keep us away from God and from the ones we have offended.
- An exile is not the best place to be in and some today are in the prison, to be locked up and separated from their families some for life, some for years or months for their offences and sin.
- Pray with child for the forgiveness of his/her sins.
- Encourage the child to live for God and all that is good and Godly from now on.

Parent/Teacher's additional note:

Parents/Teachers Manual

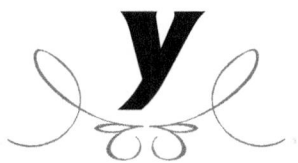

Y is for yeast, used in making bread.

Read: Luke 13:20-21 (The Message Bible)

Points:

- To make or bake bread we need some things like flour, water, pinch of salt, some sugar and some yeast.
- The yeast is so tiny and in grains.
- The yeast gets melted in warm water and is added to the flour at some point in the preparation.
- Tiny as it is, the yeast works quietly on the flour and makes it to increase greatly in size over some time.
- Sin is very tiny and cannot be seen most times yet when it is not confessed it can work quietly on a person to destroy their health, wealth, family, work and testimony.

Exercise:

- Show the child some grains of yeast if available or check it out at the shops in your next outing.
- If you can, bake some bread with the child giving a helping hand using some yeast.
- Alternatively visit a nearby bakery for child to see what happens there.

- Explain to the child what sin is – doing what is wrong or not doing what is right.
- Identify a few sins peculiar to child's age and child and explain why it is wrong e.g. telling lies is breaking God's law, hurts Mum and Dad and makes it difficult for them to belief the child. Stealing is taking what belongs to someone else without asking therefore denying them of its use and breaking God's law. If uncontrolled, the child could grow up stealing and be put in jail for a long time or for life.
- Together with child, identify one wrongdoing or action or behaviour of the child and identify ways the child can overcome this wrong behaviour or habit e.g. telling lies – identify why the child prefers to tell lies and not the truth, make child aware that God knows everything so there is no need to lie. Child should learn to tell the truth no matter what – especially to parents so they can know how to support him/her and also so they can trust him/her, a lie usually needs more lies to cover the first lie so it is not worth it and no liar will go to heaven [1Corinthians 6:9-10].
- Encourage the child to learn to do and say what is right always. Let the child know that this is possible with God's help.

Parents/Teachers Manual

Parent/Teacher's additional note:

Z is for Zion, the hill upon which God said there shall be deliverance and in which God dwells.

Read: 2 Samuel 5:7; Isaiah 8:18

Points:

- Mount Zion is located within Jerusalem.
- Mount Zion is also called the city of David.
- David lived in the fortified city of Mount Zion.
- The ark containing the Ten Commandments was kept in Mount Zion during the time of King David.

Exercise:

- Identify with the child where child's home is located e.g. 11, Somebody Close, Beautiful Gardens, Some town in your country.

Explain to the child:

- The equivalent of the City of David where you live e.g. the King's Palace or Aso Rock in Nigeria, Buckingham Palace in London or Whitehouse in Washington D.C in the USA etc.

- What could be expected if you visit any of the places above e.g. tight security by armed police, soldiers and protection from intruders and uninvited persons etc.
- God is our greatest security and He is everywhere.
- Encourage the child to learn to trust God for his/her protection everywhere and every day.

Well done parent/teacher. Good job!

May the promise of God in Proverbs 22:6 be ours in Jesus' name. Amen!

Parent/Teacher's additional note:

OPPORTUNITY TO BECOME A CHRISTIAN

Dear Father in heaven,

Thank you for the privilege of reading this book. Indeed I have sinned and come short of Your glory. I am grateful to You for sending Jesus Christ into this world to come to die on the cross of Calvary for me. I believe in my heart that Jesus Christ paid for my sins, past, present and future. I believe Jesus Christ was buried and on the third day He rose from the dead. I believe that Jesus Christ will come back again. I confess with my mouth and I accept Him now to be my Lord.

Master, Saviour, Brother, and Friend, I ask in Your mercy for the infilling of the Holy Spirit so that with His help, I can live a victorious life becoming all that You have ordained me to be in Jesus' name. I pray with thanksgiving. Amen.

If after reading this book you said the above prayer and became born-again, Congratulations! You are Born Again is a booklet for those who have done so through reading this book. It is a free booklet that we would like you to have. In it, the frequently asked questions are answered and this will get you on the way to growing in your newfound faith in God. You can download this free booklet from our website: www.protokospublishers.co.uk

You may also contact any of the organisations listed at the end of the book.

I look forward to hearing from you soon.
O. Ola–Ojo (2011)

Parents/Teachers Manual

Other Books By The Author:

Provocation, Prayer and Praise
(December 2004 & 2009)

Complimentary to The Christian and Infertility this book focuses on the story of an infertile woman in the Bible, her provocations, prayer and praise. Whatever makes you incomplete, unfulfilled, less than whom God made you to be, whatever issue of life that the enemy uses to provoke you calls for prayer.

Key features include:
- Some known medical reasons for infertility in the women.
- Why Hannah went to the house of God in spite of her barrenness.
- Is it true that the husband is much more than 10 sons to the infertile woman?
- When, where and how to address the source/cause of your provocation.
- God's part and your part in that promise.
- God is able to meet that humanly impossible need of yours.
- A time to celebrate and praise God.

Book Details:
Paperback: 128 pages
Language English
ISBN-13: 978-0-9557898-3-0

Review:
A Reader from London, 7 Jan 2006 on Amazon.co.uk
An excellent easy to read and understand book. The principles shared in this book though primarily are for those trying for a baby could as well be applied to any area of hurt and un-fulfilment.

 :www.protokospublishers.com

The Christian and Infertility
(December 2004 & 2009)

The Christian and Infertility addresses one of the often neglected needs of Christian couples. It gives an insight into infertility from the biblical and medical perspectives. It is written not only for potential fruitful couples but for pastors, family and friends of these couples. It is written that the Body of Christ might be fully equipped to know and support couples who are facing the challenge of infertility at present.

Key features include:
- Childleness in the Bible and lessons to learn;
- Some possible physical, medical and environmental causes of infertility;
- Some known spiritual causes of infertility;
- The man and low sperm count;
- Some of the available treatment options in the UK;
- Choice of fertility treatment;
- Should a christian professional be involved in fertility treatment?

Book Details:
Paperback: 146 pages
Language English
ISBN-13: 978-0-9557898-2-3

Review:
A reviewer from Glen Burnie, USA, 29 Oct 2007 on Amazon.co.uk'
The book is a great eye-opener for all. It sheds light on infertility from the medical and spiritual angle. This gives the reader a balance because i believe every human being is made up of both physical and spiritual part. To get a balance in life, the two parts must be well fed. One must not concentrate on the spiritual and neglect the physical part. The book also reminds us that God has a way of sorting us out.... The book is quite inspiring. I will recommend this book to everybody trusting God for any form of blessing from God to go get one and apply it to his or her situation. It will definitely bless you and yours'.

 :www.protokospublishers.com

Parents/Teachers Manual

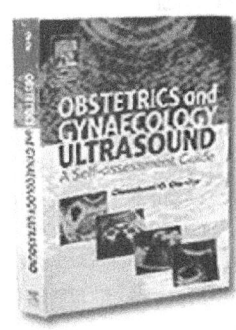

Obstetrics and Gynaecology Ultrasound -
A Self-Assessment Guide
June 2005 Churchill Elsevier Publishers, UK.

This self-assessment guide is a structured questions and answer book that develops the reader's understanding capability using a simple method in treating related topics. Clinical indications are presented with their corresponding ultrasound findings using appropriate illustrations. A case study approach is followed; presenting the clinical and ethical dilemmas that might arise whilst encouraging students to think. The aim is to reinforce theoretical knowledge within a clinical environment.

Book details:
- Over 600 high-resolution ultrasound images
- Cover a wide spectrum of ultrasound curriculum.
- Includes a detailed study of fertility.
- Aids quick understanding of subject matter.
- 468 pages.

ISBN-10: 0443064628
ISBN-13: 978-0443064623

Review:
"...This excellent new book is a study guide... This is an attractive paperback that should be essential reading for trainee obstetric and gynaecological sonographers, whether they are radiographers or radiology or obstetric trainees. It will be of particular value to those preparing for the RCOG/ RCR Diploma in Advanced Obstetric Ultrasound and to specialist registrars in obstetrics and gynaecology undertaking special skills modules in fetal medicine, gynaecological ultrasound and infertility..."

The Obstetrician & Gynaecologist, www.rcog.org.uk/togonline
Book reviews 2006

Reviewer **Ann Harper MD FRCPI FRCOG.**
Consultant Obstetrician and Gynaecologist
Royal Jubilee Maternity Service, Belfast., UK

 :www.protokospublishers.com

GOOD MUMS, BAD MUMS
(June 2005 & 2009)

This is in two parts, the main chapter that can be used for personal or group study, and an accompanying exercise section. The privileged position of a mother is in her being a co-creator with God and bringing forth life (lives). This book compliments one of God's previous revelations to me as contained in the book titled Good Dads, Bad Dads'. While the father could be likened to the pilot of the family plane, the mother can be likened to the force behind the plane – positive or negative. Good mothers are not only co-creators with God, they also do nurture as well as nourish their children physically, emotionally and spiritually.

Keys Features:
- Were all the mothers in the Bible good mothers?
- Lessons from the strengths and weakness of seven mothers.
- Be encouraged - you are not alone in the assignment of motherhood.
- Be motivated in the areas of your strengths.
- Learn ways of supporting your husband and children.

Book Details:
Paperback: 162 pages
Language English
ISBN-13: 978-0-9557898-1-6

Review:
I appreciate the author's method of writing. It is always exciting holding her book to read. Personally, 'Good Mums, Bad Mums' has been a blessing to me in no small measure. The book is rich, it is loaded with physical and spiritual uplifting subjects. To all existing and potential mothers, this book is a MUST read. At the end of every chapter there is an exercise to do that will help in re-examining your life spiritually and in other ways. I encourage all women to get and use this book as a guide in raising their children. You will be glad you did.

Pastor Mrs T Adegoke
Freedom Arena
London, UK

 :www.protokospublishers.com

Parents/Teachers Manual

To the Bride with Love
(2007 & 2009)

Every wise woman preparing to get married knows she will need sound advice, practical tips and solid, heartfelt prayers, of those who have travelled on the road she is about to journey on. In this book, 10 women of different age groups, from different backgrounds and cultures who wedded under various circumstances, individually share their experience with the bride in an intimate, very candid and unforgettable way.

Book details:
Paperback: 108 pages
Language English
ISBN-13: 978-0-9557898-4-7

To the Bride with Love is the perfect bride's evergreen companion. The content is suitable, relevant and applicable even decades after the wedding day.

To the Bride with Love is an ideal wedding gift on its own. It can also accompany any other gift (big or small) that you have for the bride but take this hint… the bride will keep thanking you for the book years and years after.

Reviews:
'One of the best', 19 Jul 2008 on Amazon.com
Sade Olaoye "clare4good" (United Kingdom)
This book has really helped my marriage from the onset as I got it as a wedding gift, God bless the giver. It's a must read for relationship improvement and God's guidance. I recommend it for people to get it for themselves, moreover as a great blessing for someone else in love. "To the Bride with Love"

Review by **Oyinlola Odunlami** CEO.
Shallom Bookshop, London UK
The writing style of Oluwakemi is unique, peculiar and distinct to herself. I recommend To the Bride with Love to wives, wives to be, mothers, mentors, youth leaders and workers. Why? The clarity, the focus and the intent of this book is so empowering, encouraging and enlightening that it will definitely mould or re mould a life to achieve its purpose. The truth is, there are very few

books that have depth as well as help you to achieve your goals and arrive at your destination. Many books tend to excite you but have no depth; you read and you forget; they do not really change you but this book, To the Bride with Love will definitely leave a word in your spirit and move you to your next level!

I believe that this is also a book that pastors will find useful as a manual for marriage counselling, because many books on marriage focus mostly on what you as an individual can gain, your own personal satisfaction while little is said about the sacrifices involved and their importance. As my pastor usually says, it is important to learn from those who have gone ahead, understand why some were successful and others weren't, so that we won't fall where they fell, rather, we would gain more speed, achieve our goals and thereby glorify Christ.

So, I invite you not only to get a copy of this life-changing manual for yourself, but also to put it into as many hands as you can afford to, for then the world will definitely benefit and your life will be a blessing to many.

:www.protokospublishers.com

Parents/Teachers Manual

Refuge Under His Wings

"an exhaustive analysis of the Book of Ruth in the Bible. The author combines her deep Christian conviction and excellent knowledge of the Holy Scriptures to produce a must read for every Christian, married or single. The book is interspaced with beautifully written prayers, which enables the reader to pause, pray and meditate on the revelations received... The book is also loaded with poetry like 'Thy will be done oh Lord' for those who may be facing an uncertain future or on a cross road of decisions."

Dr E B Ekpo MD, FRCP
Queen Elizabeth Hospital, Christian Fellowship,
Woolwich, London. UK

"...[a] ...spiritually sound book... a fine work of thoughtful reading and study... I therefore recommend it to every Christian, married or single....
Pat Roach Senior Pastor
New Covenant Church.
Wandsworth Branch, London. UK.

Book details:
Paperback: 100 pages
Language English
ISBN-10: 095578980X
ISBN-13: 978-0955789809

Review:
This book feeds the soul. Most of all I loved the poetry. It gives you time to savour the thoughts as a reader. There is a good mix of poetry and prose. To look at the story of Ruth in depth gave good spiritual food. You can pause and take it in at your own pace. The meditation on Psalm 121 was good also. There's nothing like reading a Psalm slowly and meditating on its contents. The author's own reflections allow you to see the book through someone else's eyes. A good read.

Gaby Richards, London, UK.

 :www.protokospublishers.com

GRACE OR WORKS

This book makes you examine a lot of issues in your life, family relationships in particular, that you may have taken for granted or totally ignored. As conveyed right from the rhetorical question posed in the title, Grace or Works, the author stirs you towards asking yourself pertinent questions, thinking through for answers and even getting solutions for unresolved problems.

Have you heard of prodigal wives, husbands, mothers or prodigal fathers? This book identifies and defines them clearly. For anyone experiencing a crises in their relationship with such prodigal family members, this book, which is based on the parable of the "Prodigal son" in Luke 15:11-32 is a one-stop resource material to meet your counselling needs. And just in case you happen to be the prodigal who has caused your relatives much sorrow, there is hope for you in this book.

Interspersed with prayers for you by the author and specific prayers that you can say for yourself, as well as poems to comfort and inspire you, Grace or Works not only asks you questions, it helps you make and maintain the right choices.

Book details:
Paperback: 122 pages
Language English
ISBN-13: 978-0-9557898-5-4

 :www.protokospublishers.com

Parents/Teachers Manual

THERE IS A REWARD FOR PARENTING

Man may claim that the conception of a particular child was accidental, but in God's eyes every child is in His plan and has a purpose and mission to fulfil here on earth. As a parent, teacher, church or community leader, how are you treating the children in your care?

God does not sleep nor slumber; are you sure you are doing what He expects of you as a parent or children's Sunday school teacher? What kind of reward do you expect from Him?

There is a Reward for Parenting provides a lot of answers and food for thought, using scriptural principles to show you how to ensure a good reward from God in the unique assignment of parenting and child care.

As characteristic of Oluwakemi Ola-Ojo's previous books, there is a free gift of her poems at the end of this book also, to add value to the content of the main text – making it two books for the price of one!

Book details:
Paperback: 88 pages
Language English
ISBN 978-0-9557898-6-1

Review:
The book is lovely, inspiring, very educative both spiritually and secularly.

M.F.Owoeye
Lagos- Nigeria

 :www.protokospublishers.com

Let's Reason Together ...Youths' A-Z (Book 1)

According to the United Nations demographic statistics, the global youth population, ranging in age from 15 to 24 years, today stands at more than 1.5 billion, representing about 22 percent or a fifth of the world's 6.8 billion people inhabiting the earth. In developing nations where a greater number of this group resides, the youth population sometimes gets as high as 60% or more of the total population of such nations!

Since it is also globally accepted that the youth of any nation forms the strength of that nation, economically, militarily and/or otherwise, it is imperative that this group of people cannot be overlooked.

It is against this backdrop that the book, **LET'S REASON TOGETHER – YOUTH'S A-Z** is a timely one that is set to address the various issues that affect young people as well as their vision and aspirations. Since the primary goal of young people is to live full lives in their societies, this book examines specific elements that would help them in this process. It covers a wide range of issues from the sublime such as attitude, choices, education, health and xenophobia to the seemingly mundane such as dreams, integrity and vacation etc.

Oluwakemi Ola-Ojo has written from her wealth of experience both in the medical field as well as from a spiritual point of view and it is evident that a lot of research work was put into writing this book. Irrespective of your age and/or religious persuasion, this book will inform and guide you.

Book details:
Paperback: 316 pages
Language English
ISBN 978-0-9557898-7-8

Reviews:
This is the most wonderful piece of youth work I have ever seen, capturing diverse situations and circumstances peculiar to youths. The work is thorough, educative and spiritually exhilarating. It is a must have for every youth worker to use, either in group discussions, seminars or straightforward teaching. This piece of work will yet raise the gospel abroad.
Dr M Akindele, Consultant Paediatrician, London, UK

Parents/Teachers Manual

This is a must read for the youths and anyone that deals with teenagers. All Sunday school staff will benefit from this book.
Deaconess B. Josiah. London, UK

:www.protokospublishers.com

Let's Reason Together ...Youths' A-Z (Book 2)

According to the United Nations demographic statistics, the global youth population, ranging in age from 15 to 24 years, today stands at more than 1.5 billion, representing about 22 percent or a fifth of the world's 6.8 billion people inhabiting the earth. In developing nations where a greater number of this group resides, the youth population sometimes gets as high as 60% or more of the total population of such nations!

Since it is also globally accepted that the youth of any nation forms the strength of that nation, economically, militarily and/or otherwise, it is imperative that this group of people cannot be overlooked.

It is against this backdrop that the book, LET'S REASON TOGETHER – YOUTH'S A-Z is a timely one that is set to address the various issues that affect young people as well as their vision and aspirations. Since the primary goal of young people is to live full lives in their societies, this book examines specific elements that would help them in this process. It covers a wide range of issues from the sublime such as anger, drugs, examination, homosexuality, jealousy and rejection to the seemingly mundane such as growth, ignorance and youth etc.

Oluwakemi Ola-Ojo has written from her wealth of experience both in the medical field as well as from a spiritual point of view and it is evident that a lot of research work was put into writing this book.

Irrespective of your age and/or religious persuasion, this book will inform and guide you. I recommend it to youths as well as parents and every person working with young people i.e. Sunday school teachers, youth leaders and pastors and social workers.

Book details:
Paperback: 322 pages
Language English
ISBN 978-0-9557898-9-2

 :www.protokospublishers.com

GOOD DADS, BAD DADS

This is a timeless book for men of all generations. It is very pragmatic, informative and honest in its outlook and aims to be some resource of great support and guidance to fathers specifically and men in general.

It tackles such issues as showing favouritism, unconditional love, keeping pledges, providing for the family, building an altar of worship, obedience to God's voice and the importance of leadership in the home among others.

It is a very good indicator for men who want to ensure that peace, love and orderliness reign supreme in their homes and all other endeavours of life they are involved in. It is by no means exhaustive in its nature but acts as a pointer to the ageless truths found in the Bible. It challenges men to be all that they can be for the good of the society they live in and most of all the best fathers any children may ever desire to have. It is based on some Biblical characters, all of whom are very different one from the other with their flaws and areas of excellence in order that the good father today might eschew their short-comings and pursue those aspects of these biblical characters that are worthy.

To ensure that fathers continually transform their lives, there is an accompanying workbook to stimulate them and to keep the nuggets found in this book close to their hearts which in turn reflects in the way they live their lives.

Book details:
Paperback: 230 pages
Language English
ISBN 978-1-908015-00-6

"Just a note to say that the book 'Good Dads Bad Dads' is a powerful and thought-provoking book".

Prof A. I. Sodeye - United Kingdom

"To start with, I find the book pleasurable to read and understand. In my opinion the book is prophetic in that for individuals who are spiritually inclined, there is a conviction in a way that as you read along you tend to feel that this is not just a book discussing a topic.

The book is very engaging. It provides avenue for readers to reflect and take stock as they read along. Not only that, as a pastor I realise that most of the fatherly problems were highlighted maturedly though factually. The author provides us the opportunity to receive fresh insights from what is practicable and on-going in human affairs - duties and responsibilities of fathers. Additionally the book is timely in that we have many absent-fathers presently, which if they were opportuned to read or hear from someone who had read the book, at least the number of the run-away fathers, or absentees could have reduced.

The book is filled with wisdom and encouragement for anyone doing well as a father, simultaneously for those who are not really there yet, hope, contact details and prayers of repentance are offered.

I salute the author for being able to communicate effectively on a sensitive topic such as this one. The book, Good dads, Bad dads is not judgemental or sentimental, but is one of the books which is culturally relevant and once read, you will like to read it again."

Pastor Isaac Ajibolorunrin,
Christ The Lord Tabernacle, UK

 :www.protokospublishers.com

GOOD DADS, BAD DADS (Work Book)

This is a timeless book for men of all generations. It is very pragmatic, informative and honest in its outlook and aims to be some resource of great support and guidance to fathers specifically and men in general.

It tackles such issues as showing favouritism, unconditional love, keeping pledges, providing for the family, building an altar of worship, obedience to God's voice and the importance of leadership in the home among others.

It is a very good indication for men who want to ensure that peace, love and orderliness reign supreme in their homes and all other endeavours of life they are involved in. It is not at all exhaustive in its nature but acts as a pointer to the ageless truths found in the Bible. It challenges men to be all that they can be for the good of the society they live in and most of all the best fathers any children may ever desire to have.

To ensure that fathers continually transform lives, this is the accompanying workbook to stimulate them and to keep the nuggets found close to their hearts which in turn reflects in the way they live their lives.

Book details:
Paperback: 152 pages
Language English
ISBN 978-1-908015-01-3

Parents/Teachers Manual

ABC of PEOPLE and THINGS in the BIBLE

This Workbook 'ABC of People and Things in the Bible' is specifically written for the 6-8 year old as a corresponding tool to help the child learn and practice the lessons taught from the book, ABC of People and Things in the Bible. It provides a series of basic do-it-yourself activities such as reading, writing and drawing.

The workbook is a perfect teaching aid that enables the child to express him/herself and helps the parent/teacher to identify the depth of the child's understanding or otherwise of the lessons taught.

Book details:
Paperback: 64 pages
Language English
ISBN 978-1-908015-05-1

 :www.protokospublishers.com

ABC of PEOPLE and THINGS in the BIBLE
(Parent/Teachers Manual 1)

Creative! That is the only word to describe Oluwakemi Ola-Ojo's new book, ABC of People and Things in the Bible. Many Christian parents desire to give their children an early start in Christian living and discipline through the knowledge of the Bible but simply do not know how. The reason for this is not farfetched. Teaching a six-year old is not exactly a dinner date, or is it?

ABC of People and Things in the Bible provides the perfect answer to this challenge. The book presents a highly efficient way of teaching 6-8 year-olds the Bible in a friendly yet educative manner. Using the letters of the English alphabet, Oluwakemi Ola-Ojo details the lives of people in the Bible, to teach children moral values that will help to shape their lives as well as helping them to identify and avoid mistakes that destroyed the lives of some of the characters mentioned.

The book comes highly recommended as a teaching aid not just in Sunday school but in regular school classes as well as private home studies.

Book details:
Paperback: 112 pages
Language: English
ISBN 978-1-908015-04-4

Parents/Teachers Manual

COMING OUT SOON

- **ABC OF PEOPLE AND THINGS IN THE BIBLE BOOK 2 SERIES**
- **ABC OF PLACES AND THINGS IN THE BIBLE BOOK 2 SERIES**

USEFUL ADDRESSES & WEBSITES

Care for the Family
PO Box 488
Cardiff
CF15 7YY
Tel: (029) 2081 0800
Fax: (029) 2081 4089
Email: mail@cff.org.uk
Website: www.care-for-the-family.org.uk OR www.cff.org.uk
Care for the Family aims to promote strong family life and to help those hurting because of family breakdown. Their heart is to come alongside people in the good times and in the tough times – bringing hope, compassion and some practical, down-to-earth help and encouragement.

Children Evangelism Ministry Inc
P.O. Box 4480
Ilorin, Kwara State,
Nigeria.
Tel: +234 31 222199
E-mail: cem@ilorin.skannet.com OR cem562000@yahoo.com
Children Evangelism Ministry Inc is a ministry that reaches out with the Gospel to children before and after birth. The ministry teaches and equips parents, teachers and coordinators of Sunday Schools and Children's Clubs. They also have and hold Children's Clubs, conferences and training seminars.

Focus on the Family
Tel: 1-800 - 232 6459
Website: www.family.org
Focus on the Family cooperates with the Holy Spirit in disseminating the Gospel of Jesus Christ to as many people as possible, and, specifically, to accomplish that objective by helping to preserve traditional values and the institution of the family.

Protokos Publishers
P.O. Box 48424
London
SE15 2YL
www.protokospublishers.co.uk

Protokos Publishers provides various resources for the family. We publish many life's enlightening, informative and motivational must read books. With each of our books, you are guaranteed a 24/7 counsellor by your side on the subject.

The Shepherd's Ministries
5 Brookehowse Road
Bellingham
London SE6 3TJ, UK
Tel/Fax: +44 208 698 7222
Email: info@theshepherdsministries.org
Website: www.theshepherdsministries.org

The Shepherd's Ministries helps to bring children into an experience of worshipping God in truth and in spirit; give children a world-view based on God's word and mission and helps children to exercise their gifts in local and global missions.

Total Woman Ministries
The Total Woman Ministries,
3 Herringham Road
Thames Wharf Barrier,
Charlton,
London
SE7 8NJ.
Tel: 020 8293 3730
Fax: 020 8293 3731
Email: admin@totalwomanministries.org
Website:www.totalwomanministries.org

Total Woman Ministries by God's grace has the sole vision of reaching out to women of all categories *(married, single, separated, divorced, young, middle-aged or elderly)*.

United Christian Broadcasting UCB
P.O. Box 255, Stoke on Trent,
ST4 8YY, England
Among other forms of spreading the Gospel, UCB prints The Word For Today – a free daily devotional reading available for residents in the UK and Republic of Ireland

IN USA:
www.eCounseling.com
Tel Number: 1-866-268-6735

Dear Reader,

Thank you for your time and resources committed to supporting this writing ministry. Please help to tell others about how much the Lord has blessed you reading this book.

You will certainly be blessed by the other books written by Oluwakemi, so why not visit www.protokospublishers.co.uk and place an order today.

It will equally be appreciated if you can help to write a few sentences review of the book on www.amazon.com and/or on www.protokospublishers.co.uk

Please note that all our books are easily available on our website and other good bookshops.

God bless you as you do.
Management
Protokos Publishers.

www.ingramcontent.com/pod-product-compliance
Lightning Source LLC
Chambersburg PA
CBHW071004080526
44587CB00015B/2342